Contents

Assembly Today
for Key Stage 1

INTRODUCTION

Coming up with new and interesting ideas for assembly can often be an extremely difficult and time consuming task. Ideally, of course, the subject matter should have a clear moral message, should be motivating to the pupils and be of a broadly Christian outlook. In this book we have created a range of assemblies for use within a wide range of schools and appropriate for all children regardless of their faith or cultural heritage.

The assemblies are arranged according to appropriate times of year in school terms, although many can be used across the whole school year as well. Each assembly has a moral or appropriate message, a visual or physical element, a prayer and a suggested song or hymn.

For most of the assemblies you will need to use an overhead projector. Where the assemblies include stories we have sometimes provided silhouettes that need to be photocopied on to paper and then cut out (before the assembly) for display on the OHP. This creates the simplest form of shadow puppet show that is certain to gain the children's full attention! For other stories a separate picture is provided that can be photocopied on to acetate and placed on the OHP to act as a visual aid while the story is being read out. For the rest of the stories we have mixed the pictures with the text. Here you can photocopy on to acetate and then present the story and text on the OHP so the children can follow the text as well as the pictures. If you have plenty of preparation time you could involve children in the retelling of the story or they could even role play the issues being addressed.

For some of the assemblies you might simply want to follow the script that is provided on the teachers' page, while for others you might want to read the assembly first and then present it in your own words. The script in italic type can be used directly or use it as the basis for your presentation. Whatever style of presentation you choose, assemblies should be an enjoyable and thought provoking experience for all concerned.

Give away a smile

AIM: To encourage children to see the value in being cheerful and friendly to others.

PREPARATION

- If you are planning to use an OHP, photocopy 'Give away a smile' (page 4) on to acetate.
- As children arrive in the hall/assembly catch the attention of just one or two children by smiling broadly at them so that they automatically return your smile.
- Wait until all the children are quietly seated before beginning the assembly.

INTRODUCTION

Introduce the assembly by saying something like:

Have you noticed how it is always more fun to be with cheerful people than with gloomy ones? Today's assembly is all about being cheerful and helping those around you to feel cheerful too.

ASSEMBLY

Ask the question:

How can you tell if people are feeling happy?

Accept a number of answers. The particular answer you are hoping to get at this stage is that if people smile you know they are happy.

Now pick out the child/children that you targeted with your smile on the way into assembly and ask them to come and stand with you.

Ask the question:

What happened to you on the way into assembly today?

If you smiled broadly enough they should be able to tell you that you smiled at them.

What did you do when I smiled at you?

They will hopefully realise that they returned the smile.

Ask the rest of the children:

Why did ____________ smile at me when I smiled at him/her/them?

Use this question to uncover the fact that it is automatic to return a smile. Ask the 'target' child/children to return to their places.

REFLECTION

When you smile at someone it tells them that you are friendly and it makes them feel happy. The more we smile at one another the more cheerful everyone ends up feeling. Perhaps today in school you could try smiling at people as you meet them. It would be particularly good if you smiled at someone that you don't usually get on well with – you might even make some new friends this way.

Prayer

Dear God,
Help me to remember the importance of my smile.
Throughout the day at school keep me cheerful all the while.
Whether I am working, or if I am at play
Help me pass my smile around to others through this day.
Amen

Song Magic penny (Alleluya, 10: *A&C Black*)

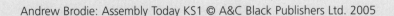

Give away a smile

We are all special

 AIM: To encourage pupils to feel self confident members of the school community.

PREPARATION

■ If you are planning to use an OHP, photocopy 'We are all special' (page 6) on to acetate and cut into separate pictures.

▥ INTRODUCTION

Who thinks they are usually kind? (Show of hands.) Who thinks they are good at... reading, numeracy, etc. Who thinks they are good at sports? Today you are going to hear a story about a boy who thought he wasn't very good at anything.

▥ STORY

Share the following story with the children:

Michael was a little boy in year two at Fieldford School. He enjoyed going to school each day but felt sad that he wasn't actually very good at anything. He struggled with some of his work. No-one could tell what his paintings were meant to be and when he changed for P.E. he always seemed to end up with only one shoe. Every morning his teacher picked a name from a small plastic box, and that person was the 'special person' for the day. Michael dreaded his name being picked out as he didn't think he could possibly be special enough. (Put special person sign on OHP).

One Tuesday morning Michael's name was taken from the box. This meant that he had to go and sit outside the classroom for a short time so that the other children could tell the teacher about anything that they thought made Michael a special person. Michael didn't think he'd be there long as there wouldn't be much to say about him.

After a while Michael started to worry. Why hadn't he been called back inside? Perhaps no-one could think of anything good to say about him. Hours seemed to pass, though in fact it was only about five minutes, before, at last Michael was called into the classroom again. "Now Michael," said his teacher, "Would you like to know what your classmates said about you?" Michael wanted to say no and run away, but he found himself nodding nervously.
"You are always kind to others." (Put kind picture on OHP.)
"Whatever you are asked to do you always try your best." (Add trying hard picture to OHP.)
"You play games fairly." (Add playing fairly picture to OHP.)
"You share your things with others." (Add sharing picture to OHP.)
"You join in with all activities." (Add joining in picture to OHP.)

The list of all Michael's good qualities went on and on. By this time Michael was so happy he could hardly hear what was being said, but luckily his teacher had written down the whole, very long, list of all the things the other children had said about him so he was able to look at it later. As he went home that afternoon, clutching this very precious list, Michael knew that he was indeed very special and that he would never again worry about not being good at anything.

▥ REFLECTION

Prayer

Dear God,
Thank you for making every single one of us special. Help us all to appreciate our own good qualities, and those of everyone else in our school. Please help us to remember to try our hardest in everything we do, and to encourage others to do the same.
Amen

♫
Song   This little light of mine   (Alleluya, 14: *A&C Black*)

We are all special

Special Person

Harvesting the vegetables – the enormous turnip

 AIM: As part of the harvest celebrations to encourage children to realise that working together can be more productive than working alone.

PREPARATION

- Although this story appears in the early part of the school year it would be ideal to use in the same calendar year as the story 'Planting the seeds' that is included on page 45 in the Summer Term section of this book.
- You will need to photocopy and cut out the silhouettes on page 9 ready to use at appropriate points in this assembly. You may also like to use some of the silhouettes from the Summer Term 'Planting the seeds' (page 46).
- If available, a turnip would be an excellent visual aid.

INTRODUCTION

At this time of year the days are getting shorter and the nights are getting longer. The weather is getting colder, some of the flowers are dying, the leaves on the trees are beginning to change colour ready to fall off for the winter. Now is the time when farmers get very busy with the harvest, gathering in the crops that have grown throughout the summer. Lots of gardeners are very busy too. They have had flowers to look at all summer and now the flowers are dying back so they have to tidy up the flower beds. They may be collecting in vegetables and fruit they have grown as well. Our story today is about a gardener called Eric who planted seeds in his garden back in April or May.

STORY

Share this story with the children:

Eric loved to work in his garden. One particular day, Eric decided to plant some vegetable seeds. He planted carrot seeds, pea seeds, bean seeds but, most importantly, he planted turnip seeds because he loved turnips. After he had planted the seeds, he gave them all a small amount of water from his watering can. Some days it was sunny and some days there was rain. Warmth from the sun and water from the rain are exactly what seeds need to help them grow.

Day after day, Eric looked after the seeds. Then, one day, he became very excited because he saw some little tiny green leaves beginning to appear from out of the soil. Day after day, he looked after the little leaves and they grew bigger and stronger. His seeds were growing into strong healthy plants. Eric was looking forward to eating the vegetables – but he would have to wait for quite a long time because vegetables take a long time to grow. Eric was looking forward to his turnips most of all, because he loved turnips.

All through the summer Eric watched his turnip plants growing. (Place silhouette of leaves growing on to the OHP.) *Turnips grow just under the top of the soil so Eric could see the leaves and he could see the very tops of the turnips themselves. The strange thing was that one turnip was growing much bigger and stronger than all of the others. It grew and it grew and it grew. It was enormous.*

At last September came and Eric decided that it was time to enjoy eating some turnip. "I'll pull out that enormous one," he said to his wife, Peggy, and their two children, Jack and Jenny. Eric pulled on his Wellington boots and went out into the garden. He walked to his vegetable patch and there was his row of turnips with the great big enormous one in the middle. Eric caught hold of the great big enormous leaves and started to give a great big enormous pull. (Place Eric so that he appears to be pulling the largest leaves.) *But he just couldn't pull that turnip out – it was too enormous.*

Eric sat down for a rest, then decided that he would need some help. He walked back to the house and called in through the back door,
"Peggy, can you help me for a minute?"

Harvesting the vegetables – the enormous turnip

So Peggy went out into the garden with Eric. Eric caught hold of the turnip leaves and Peggy caught hold of Eric. They pulled really hard but the great big enormous turnip just wouldn't move. (Place Peggy so that she appears to be pulling on Eric's waist.)
"We need more help," said Peggy. "I'll go and fetch Jack."
"But he's only eight," said Eric.
"Every little helps," replied Peggy.
Peggy went off up the garden path. Eric looked at his turnip and his mouth watered at the thought of the tasty turnip stew that he would cook later.

Soon Peggy and Jack arrived at the vegetable patch. Eric caught hold of the turnip leaves, Peggy caught hold of Eric and Jack caught hold of Peggy. (Add Jack to the picture.) *They pulled really hard but the great big enormous turnip just wouldn't move.*
"We need more help," said Eric. "I'll go and fetch Jenny."
"But she's only five," said Jack.
"Every little helps," replied Eric.

Eric went off up the garden path. Peggy stood looking at the enormous turnip thinking how tasty it would be. Jack stood looking at the enormous turnip thinking how he didn't like vegetables and he especially didn't like this one because he wanted to go inside to watch television.

Soon Eric and Jenny arrived at the vegetable patch. Eric caught hold of the turnip leaves, Peggy caught hold of Eric, Jack caught hold of Peggy and Jenny caught hold of Jack. (Add Jenny to the picture.) *They pulled really hard, then they pulled again really hard, then the turnip began to move.*
"One more time," called Eric.
They all pulled really hard again then, suddenly, out popped the turnip. Eric and Peggy and Jack and Jenny all tumbled over backwards, laughing and shouting.
"Well done everybody," cried Eric. "You see what happens when everybody works together!"
They carried the enormous turnip into the house where Eric cut it up and cooked a wonderful turnip stew. Even Jack liked it.

▥ REFLECTION

What is the moral of the story? What does the story teach us?

Hopefully the children will be able to respond with appropriate suggestions, perhaps incorporating the ideas that 'every little helps' and 'jobs are much easier if everybody works together'.

Prayer

Dear God,
Help us all to help each other. Help us to remember that jobs are much easier to do if everybody works together.

Amen

Song

With a little help from my friends   (Alleluya, 38: *A&C Black*)

Andrew Brodie: Assembly Today KS1 © A&C Black Publishers Ltd. 2005

Harvesting the vegetables – the enormous turnip

Falling leaves

 AIM: To help children to be aware of the seasons and to nuture feelings of wonder about changes in the natural world through the seasons.

PREPARATION

- To prepare for this assembly gather a collection of leaves of different shapes and sizes. These can be placed on the OHP to make very effective silhouettes.
- Alternatively you can photocopy the leaf shapes on page 11 on to acetate.

INTRODUCTION

This is intended to be a short but very interactive assembly with much use of questions and answers.

Place a leaf on the OHP so that the silhouette appears on the screen or you can use the leaf shapes on page 11.

ASSEMBLY

The suggested questions are as follows.

What is this?
Where do you think I found it?
Where do you normally find leaves?
Why was this one on the ground?
What is happening to the leaves on the trees at the moment?
What do we call this season?
Do you know what American people call this season?
Why do you think they call it the fall?
What happens to the leaves that have fallen off the trees?
What happens to the trees in the winter?
What happens in the spring?
What are trees like in the summer?
We are in the autumn now. What is the next season?
What season comes after winter?
What season comes after spring?
What season comes after summer? Yes we come back to autumn again.

REFLECTION

Prayer

Dear God,
We thank you for the seasons: Autumn, winter, spring, summer.
We thank you for the trees and the beautiful leaves that grow on them.
                                              Amen

Song

Look for signs that summer's done   (Someone's Singing, Lord, 54: *A&C Black*)

Falling leaves

How our place of worship is made

AIM: This assembly should promote the idea that the most important element of a place of worship is the people who attend.

PREPARATION

- Before the beginning of the assembly you may wish to draw a simple outline of a local place of worship on an acetate sheet for use with an OHP. (If you are a confident artist you could draw the outline during the assembly.)
- You will also need to photocopy on to acetate 'How our place of worship is made' (page 13) and cut out the separate faces.

■ INTRODUCTION

Today we are going to think about what the Church/Synagogue/Temple (substitute an alternative place of worship as appropriate) *is made of.*

What do you think?

Accept all ideas offered.

■ ASSEMBLY

I am going to ask some of you to help me to make a _____ picture, and we are going to build our picture out of the most important materials. Who would like to help me?

Choose as many children as you have shapes to put on the outline. How many you use will depend on the outline you have drawn. Give each child a shape rather secretively, encouraging them NOT to show them to the rest of the children sitting in the assembly.

Now you can take turns to add your shape to the picture so that we can build a _____ .

Allow time for the children to place their shapes in the outline and return to their places.

■ REFLECTION

The _____ is really made out of people. I know that on the outside we can see bricks or stone or wood, but the most important part of any _____ is the group of people who worship there.

If there is time you may wish to expand a little on this, pointing out that people can get together anywhere to worship, even outside, and that a place of worship without people in it has no use.

Prayer

Dear God,
Help us to live our lives in a constructive way. Building our lives with love and peace in our hearts. Caring for those around us, and accepting their beliefs and ideas.
Amen

Song

Somebody greater   (Come and Praise, 5: *BBC Books*)

How our place of worship is made

Autumn fires

AIM: To reflect on the colours of autumn and to give thanks for the beauty of the natural world.

PREPARATION

■ If you are planning to use an OHP, photocopy 'Autumn fires' (page 15) on to acetate. Alternatively you could make an enlarged paper version of the sheet.

▦ INTRODUCTION

Today we are going to think about the colours around us as the summer is gradually changing to autumn. First we are going to look at a poem about a garden bonfire that is burning in a garden in the autumn.

Here you may wish to discuss what sort of things might need to be burned from the garden, and also to reinforce the safety aspect of being near a fire.

▦ ASSEMBLY

Place the 'Autumn fires' poem on the OHP or an have enlarged paper version ready for pupils to see.

At this stage you could read the poem to the children, or you may prefer to ask a few of them to read it aloud with you.

Look at the first verse. Which word does 'trail' rhyme with?

Accept pupils' responses and explain that a vale is a valley or an area of land between hills.

Now look at the third verse. Which word rhymes with 'all'?

Accept responses and explain that the word 'fall' is the American name for autumn.

Why do you think that the Americans call autumn the fall? It's because it's the time when the leaves fall off the trees.

▦ REFLECTION

What colours did the poem make you think of?

Accept and discuss responses focusing on the appreciation of the colours around us in the natural world.

Any chance you get today, have a look at the autumn colours we are starting to notice around the school.

Accept and discuss responses focusing on the appreciation of the colours around us in the natural world.

Prayer

Dear God,
Thank you for the colours of autumn that we can see around us: the golden brown of the falling leaves, the red and yellow autumn flowers, the silver of the harvest moon and the gold of the ripe corn in the fields.

Amen

Song

Look for signs that summer's done   (Someone's Singing, Lord, 54: *A&C Black*)

Autumn fires

Autumn fires

In the other gardens
And all up the vale,
From the autumn bonfires
See the smoke trail!

Pleasant summer over,
And all the summer flowers,
The red fire blazes,
The grey smoke towers.

Sing a song of seasons!
Something bright in all!
Flowers in the summer,
Fires in the fall!

Robert Louis Stevenson

Travelling

AIM: To encourage the children to reflect thoughtfully and to consider the needs of others, specifically people who are travelling.

PREPARATION

- Prepare for the assembly by photocopying 'Travelling' (page 17) on to acetate.
- This assembly should be very calm and quiet.

▣ INTRODUCTION

Sometimes when I am busy working I like to stop for a short rest. I can't stop for long because I have a lot of work to do but I do stop for just a minute. I don't disturb anybody else because they have work to do too and they can have little rests when they want to. I just stop quietly and I find that it helps me to think.

▣ ASSEMBLY

Let's all stop now, just for a minute, and think quietly to ourselves. When it's very quiet you can sometimes hear things that you don't normally notice. Can you hear anything now?

Sometimes when I stop I like to look out of the window. Sometimes I like to look up at the sky. What do you think I see?

I see clouds, I sometimes see blue sky, I sometimes see birds. Sometimes I see aeroplanes on their journeys.

Where do you think the aeroplanes are coming from? Where do you think the aeroplanes are travelling to? (Place aeroplane picture on OHP.)

Sometimes I wish that I was on the aeroplane. I wonder where the people are going to and I wish that I was going with them.

Who do you think might be travelling on the aeroplane?

Hopefully the children will suggest the pilot and the passengers and some may be aware of other members of the crew.

Can you think of other ways that people travel?

Hopefully the children will suggest travelling by road in cars, lorries, buses; travelling by sea; travelling on trains.

▣ REFLECTION

Let's think today about all the people who are travelling. Some people are travelling short distances and some are travelling long distances, perhaps from one side of the world to the other.

Prayer

Dear God,
Help all people who are travelling today. Help them to be safe and to enjoy their journeys.
Amen

Now, let's just sit quietly and think about people who are travelling today.

♫
Song

The journey of life   (Someone's Singing, Lord, 28: *A&C Black*)

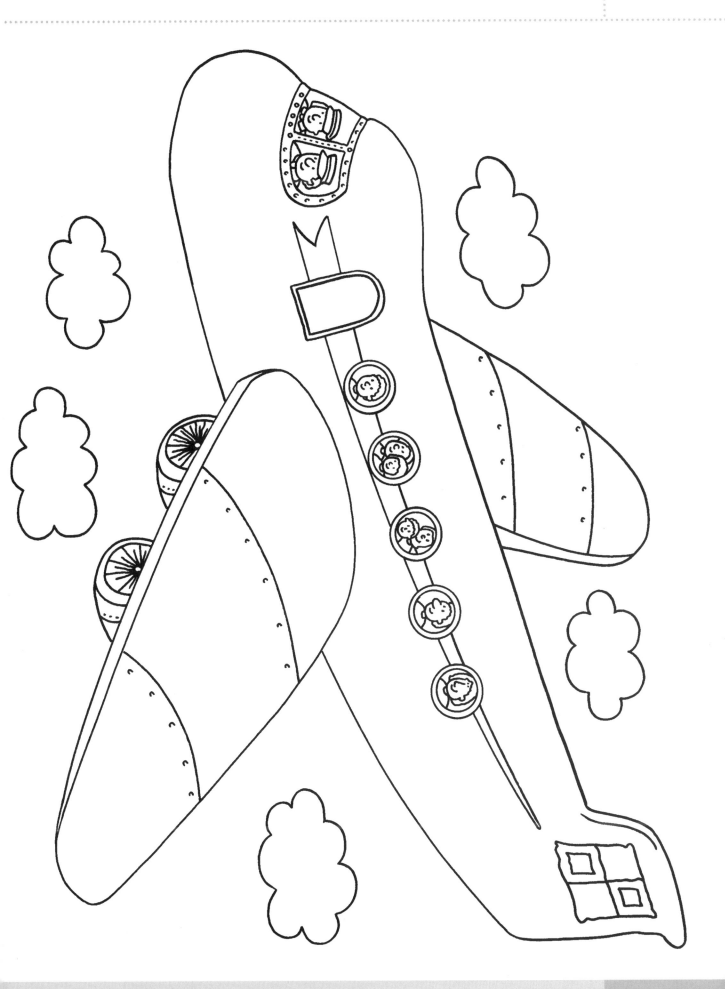

Valuing your friends 1

 AIM: To promote friendship and the appreciation of good friends, using Aesop's fable of the jackdaws.

PREPARATION

- Prepare for this assembly by photocopying and cutting out the silhouettes of the jackdaws and the crows (page 19).
- The jackdaw silhouettes should be placed on the OHP as appropriate during the story.

INTRODUCTION

A person who has good friends is a very lucky person, but it's not just luck because that person is probably a good friend too.
What makes someone a good friend?
What do good friends do for each other?
So good friends are people who look after each other; they value each other. I'm going to tell you a very old story about valuing friends.

STORY

There was once a group of jackdaws. Do you know what jackdaws are? (Place pictures of three jackdaws on OHP.)

One of the jackdaws was bigger than all the others and because of this he thought he was better than all the others too. (Add picture of larger jackdaw.) *He decided that the other jackdaws weren't good enough for him. They weren't good enough to be his friends. He left them and went off to join the crows.* (Remove all pictures. Add picture of larger jackdaw flying.)

The crows were bigger birds than the jackdaws so when the big jackdaw came to join them he didn't look very big any more. (Add picture of crows.)
"What do you want?" said the crows. "What are you doing here? We don't want you. Go away."
And they started pecking him and chasing him so he had no choice but to fly away. He flew back to the jackdaws.

"I'm back!" said the big jackdaw to the other jackdaws, as though they should be pleased to see him. (Remove crows and add all other jackdaws.)

"What do you want?" said the jackdaws. "What are you doing here? You didn't want us so we don't want you. Go away." The big jackdaw went and sat in a tree all on his own. He realised what a fool he had been. He should have stayed with his friends and not thought that he was better than them just because he was bigger. (Remove jackdaws leaving the large flying jackdaw on its own.)

REFLECTION

Prayer

Dear God,
Please help us to value our friends. Help us to be good friends to other people.
                                                                              Amen

Song   When I needed a neighbour   (Someone's Singing, Lord, 35: *A&C Black*)

    Andrew Brodie: Assembly Today KS1 © A&C Black Publishers Ltd. 2005

Valuing your friends 2

AIM: To encourage children to appreciate their friends by considering a story about people of their own age.

PREPARATION

- You may like to put the silhouettes of the jackdaws (page 19) on the OHP again for this assembly.
- Photocopy 'Valuing your friends 2' (page 22) on to an acetate sheet.

INTRODUCTION

Do you remember the story of the big jackdaw who left his friends because he thought he was too good to mix with them? Do you remember what I said at the start of that assembly? I said that a person who has good friends is a very lucky person, but it's not just luck because that person is probably a good friend too. Good friends are people who look after each other; they value each other.

The jackdaw story is a very old story. Today I'm going to tell you a very new story about valuing friends. Today's story is about somebody who behaved in exactly the same way as the big jackdaw. The story is about a girl called Nell. (If there is a 'Nell' in your school you may wish to change the name to one that does not belong to any of your pupils.)

STORY

Nell was in Year One. Her birthday was in September so she was the oldest person in her class. She was also the biggest person in her class. She was the oldest, the biggest…and she thought she was the best. She didn't want to play with the other people in her class.

At break time, Nell didn't join in with the games that the Year One children were playing. She wanted to join in with Year Two. She found some Year Two children who were playing football. She wanted to join in so she kicked the ball. But it didn't go where she thought it would go. It went completely in the wrong direction and landed in a puddle.

"Go away," said the Year Two children who were playing football. "We don't want you. You're in Year One. Go away!"

She found some Year Two children who had a skipping rope. They were very good at skipping.

"Do you want to try?" asked one of the Year Two children. Nell tried, but she got caught in the rope and fell over. Some of the Year Two children laughed at her.

"Go away," they said. "You're not in Year Two. You're only in Year One. We don't want you. Go away!"

Nell wandered off, trying to look as though she didn't mind but really she felt very upset. She saw some people from her own Year One class. 'Perhaps I can play with them,' she thought.

"Can I play with you?" asked Nell.

"NO!" they shouted. "We've got enough people in our game. Anyway, you wanted to play with Year Two. You didn't want to play with us."

Sometimes, teachers can be very clever. Nell's teacher had seen everything that had happened. She had a quiet word with Nell and she had quiet words with the Year One children. She even had quiet words with the Year Two children.

The next time that Nell went out to play she had a lovely break time. She played with the Year One children from her class and they all had a great time together. She saw the Year Two children and they smiled nicely at her then carried on with their games. Nell smiled nicely back at them then carried on with her game with her very own friends from her class.

'I like Year One,' she thought to herself. 'And I'm very lucky to have good friends in my own class.'

Valuing your friends 2

 REFLECTION

You may like to complete the assembly by posing some questions to the children:

Nell thought she was very lucky to have good friends. Was she lucky?
Do you need to be lucky to have good friends or is there something more important than luck?
What do you think Nell's teacher said to her?
What do you think Nell's teacher said to the Year One children?
What do you think Nell's teacher said to the Year Two children?
Can Year One children be friendly with Year Two children?
In what way was this story similar to the story of the big jackdaw?
In what way was this story different?
I'm now going to ask you a question that I don't want you to answer,
I just want you to think about it:
Are you a good friend?

Prayer

Dear God,
Please help us all to be good friends. Help us to be kind to other people.
Help us to value our friends.

Amen

Song   Look out for loneliness   (Someone's Singing, Lord, 36: *A&C Black*)

Valuing your friends 2

Diwali and light

AIM: To promote a sense of wonder and appreciation of light and to think about the Hindu festival of Diwali.

PREPARATION

■ You can adapt the assembly to suit the background of your school and the faiths of your pupils. The hymn is a Christian hymn but is centred round the theme of the candle flame.

■ We suggest that you turn out the lights in the hall and light a candle at the front before the children enter.

INTRODUCTION

Today we are going to talk about a very special festival. It is sometimes called the festival of lights and that's why I have lit a candle. It's not a very strong light is it? It's not very bright like the electric lights we normally use in the hall but it is a very beautiful light. Look carefully at the flame: it rises straight up but if I brush my hand past it, it flickers. Of course, I mustn't put my hand too close to it because I could burn my fingers. Flames are very dangerous if we are not careful with them.

ASSEMBLY

The Hindu festival of Diwali usually takes place in October or November each year and is a celebration of the Hindu new year. Diwali is also celebrated by Sikhs and Jains. The Diwali celebration takes place throughout the country of India and it takes place in this country too amongst the Hindu and Sikh people who live here.

Diwali is also known as the festival of lights. Night time is special during the festival of Diwali because the people decorate their houses with lights. The word Diwali actually comes from an old word that means rows of lights. Some people light candles and some people have special lamps. Other people use bright electric lights. Some people like to have firework displays to celebrate Diwali.

The festival of Diwali lasts for five days. Hindu families start the day with worship then they have breakfast together. They wear their best clothes and sometimes they buy new clothes especially for Diwali. The people in the family go out together to visit relations and friends. Sometimes they give each other presents. If people have argued at any time, Diwali is the time when they make up and forget their quarrel.

REFLECTION

Let's look at the candle flame and sit quietly while we do so. Let's think about Diwali, the festival of lights. Let's think if we have argued with anybody – perhaps we can try really hard not to argue and to make up with other people that we've argued with.

Prayer
*Dear God
Please help us to learn from Diwali. Help us to learn that we should forget our arguments and make friends with other people.*
                                                                                    Amen

Song
Like a candle flame   (Everyone's Singing, Lord, 23: *A&C Black*)
(You may also like to consider the Jewish festival of Hanukah, which is celebrated by lighting the candles on a candlestick with eight branches. There is a song for Hanukah in the book 'Harlequin', 39: *A&C Black.*)

Christmas and light

AIM: To consider the significance of light as a religious symbol. To celebrate Christmas and reflect on its Christian significance.

PREPARATION

- You can adapt the assembly to suit the background of your school and the faiths of your pupils.
- We suggest that you turn out the lights in the hall and light a candle at the front before the children enter.

ASSEMBLY

Do you remember the assembly when I talked about the festival of lights? Do you remember the special name for the festival of lights?

Lots of people are getting ready for Christmas now. People are doing their Christmas shopping, making sure that they have got all the food ready. Some people are buying presents for their friends. Some people are buying a Christmas tree.

What do people put on their Christmas trees? Sometimes presents, sometimes chocolates, sometimes special decorations. Does anybody know the name for the special decorations? It's a word beginning with 'b'. (Baubles)

And what else do people put on their Christmas trees? (Lights.)

What do we see hanging above the streets when we go shopping? (Lights.)

What have some people got in their gardens? (Lights.)

What have some people got all over their houses? (Lights.)

Why all these lights? Because Christmas is a sort of festival of lights too.

Why do we put up lights at Christmas? Because they look pretty but also because we are remembering the birth of Jesus. When Jesus was a grown-up one of the things he said was, 'I am the light of the world'. He wanted people to follow him and to behave in the ways that he taught them. He taught people to be kind to each other. He taught people to be good friends. So when we put up Christmas lights we try to remember that Jesus was born at Christmas and he grew up to teach us how to be good.

REFLECTION

Let's look at the candle flame and sit quietly while we do so. Let's think about Jesus, coming into the world as a little tiny baby. Let's try to follow what Jesus taught us. Let's try hard to be kind to each other.

Prayer

Dear God,

Please help us to remember the spirit of Christmas. Christmas is the time when Jesus came into the world. Jesus said, 'I am the light of the world'. He taught us to love one another and to be kind to one another. Help us to follow the light of Jesus and to be kind to other people.

Amen

Song

Like a candle flame   (Everyone's Singing, Lord, 23: *A&C Black*)

or

Tree of light   (Sing a Christmas Cracker, 3: *A&C Black*)

Night and day

 AIM: This assembly focuses on the differences between night and day and how we accept that each night will be followed by another day.

PREPARATION

■ Photocopy 'Night and day' (page 26) or you may prefer to make an enlarged version on larger paper.

■ INTRODUCTION

What happens at the end of each day?

Accept a variety of responses – stop when you get to the desired response that night comes after each day.

That's right; at the end of each day it gets dark and we call that the night. So what happens each time the night has finished?

Look for the response that the next day begins.

Yes, each night is followed by the next day.
We are going to look at two short poems one is about the start of the day, and one is about the night time.

■ ASSEMBLY

Show the 'Time to Rise' poem. Either read this to or with the children.

How do we know that this poem is about the daytime?

Following their ideas you should be able to discuss the fact that birds wake up when the sun rises. You will also be able to look at the day time pictures that illustrate the poem.

Next display the 'Moon' poem. Read this as you did the previous poem.

What tells us that this poem is about night time?

Again follow the ideas the children have taken from both the text and the pictures.

■ REFLECTION

Aren't we lucky to know that every day the sun comes up to keep us warm and give us light. Each evening the moon and stars help give us a little light and the night creatures all enjoy coming out to live their night-time lives. We should all be thankful for our very favourite parts of the day and of the night.

Prayer

Dear God,
We thank you for giving us both day and night, and the certainty that one will follow the other. We thank you for the early mornings when the sun rises in the sky and the birds sing. We thank you too for the beauty of the sunset as the evening turns into night, with the moon and stars to shine in the darkness.

Amen

Song

Father, we thank you for the night   (Someone's Singing, Lord, 1: *A&C Black*)
or
I watch the sunrise   (Alleluya, 15: *A&C Black*)

Night and day

Time to Rise

A birdie with a yellow bill
Hopped upon the window sill
Cocked his shining eyes and said;
"Ain't you 'shamed, you sleepy-head!"

Robert Louis Stevenson

The Moon

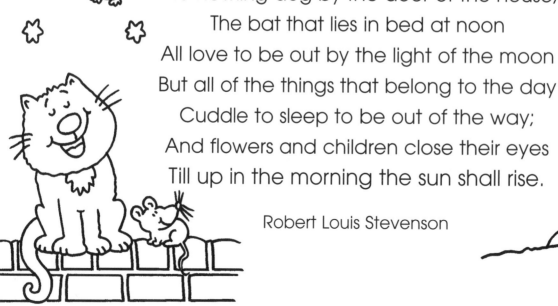

The moon has a face like the clock in the hall;
She shines on thieves on the garden wall,
On streets and fields and harbour quays,
And birdies asleep in the forks of the trees.

The squalling cat and the squeaking mouse,
The howling dog by the door of the house,
The bat that lies in bed at noon
All love to be out by the light of the moon
But all of the things that belong to the day
Cuddle to sleep to be out of the way;
And flowers and children close their eyes
Till up in the morning the sun shall rise.

Robert Louis Stevenson

Andrew Brodie: Assembly Today KS1 © A&C Black Publishers Ltd. 2005

Noah 1

 AIM: To thank God for the world around us and to ask for his help so that we may play a part in it.

PREPARATION

- If you are planning to use an OHP, photocopy 'Noah: 1 and 2' (page 29) on to acetate.
- Have coloured pens (suitable for use on acetate) available: red, orange, yellow, green, blue, indigo and violet.

INTRODUCTION

Today we are going to think about keeping promises. Who can tell us what a promise is?

Accept responses.

Who thinks they are very good at keeping promises and can tell us about a promise they have kept?

Accept responses and acknowledge the good promises among them. It is important that children learn that they should never have to keep 'bad' secrets.

I am going to tell you a story from the Bible. It has a very important promise in it.

STORY

I am going to need some helpers to do a job for me while I am reading the story.

Choose three helpers. Give each one either a pen for use on acetate, or a coloured pencil if using paper – pens/pencils should be in rainbow colours as indicated on the accompanying picture. Instruct the helpers to take turns to colour their particular band of colour on the rainbow, perhaps after each verse. Read the first part of the story of Noah's Ark:

God looked down from the heavens one day.
Why do all my people fight, not play?
They punch and kick, they shout and riot,
There is no peace, no caring, no quiet.
Perhaps it would be better to begin again
A fresh start is needed for my world of men.
God looked again at the world full of strife
And saw one good man called Noah, and his wife.
I'll save that man and his family, God thought,
As they are following the rules that I taught.

God spoke to Noah. He said, "Build a boat!"
Noah replied, "But it never will float,
Not here in the desert where the sun is high
And day after day it is always dry.
What good is a boat in this desert land
Where there is no water, only miles of sand?"
God said, "Build a boat both high and long.
Make it big and make it strong.
For soon I'm going to send some rain,
Then a sea will cover this sandy plain."

So Noah and his family got some Gopher wood
And they built an ark as God said they should.
And then on God's instruction they began to search
For every kind of animal to be found on earth.
Two Lions, two tigers and two kangaroos,
Two yaks, two bears and even two Gnus.
Two snakes slithered and two zebras ran
All heading for the ark, according to God's plan.
And just at the time when it started to pour
The last pair of creatures went in through the door.

REFLECTION

Discuss the story so far and explain that you will tell the final part of the story in the next assembly.

Prayer

Thank you Lord for the world you have given us. For all the animals, birds, fish and other living creatures on the earth. Help us to play our part in the world. Help us to be good people like Noah and his family were.

Amen

Song   Rise and shine   (Alleluya, 74: *A&C Black*)

Noah 2

AIM: To encourage children to take care of the world and to consider God's promise in the story of Noah.

PREPARATION

■ If you are planning to use an OHP, photocopy 'Noah: 1 and 2' (page 29) on to acetate and have coloured pens available. Place the partly completed rainbow from the last assembly on to the OHP.

INTRODUCTION

Do you remember the story that I was telling you last week? Do you remember that I said that there is something very special in the story? It has a very important promise in it.

STORY

I am going to need some helpers to do a job for me while I am reading the story. My helpers last week coloured part of this rainbow for me.

Choose four helpers. Give each one either a pen for use on acetate, or a coloured pencil if using paper – pens/pencils should be in rainbow colours as indicated on the accompanying picture. Instruct the helpers to take turns to colour their particular band of colour on the rainbow, after each verse, then one person should colour the final band of the rainbow to signify completing the picture. Remind the children of the story so far then read the second part of the story:

Noah and his family really didn't mind
Sharing the ark with two creatures of each kind.
It rained and rained, then rained some more.
The flood was high above the desert floor.
The rain kept raining and the ark sailed away,
Noah and his family continued to pray
To God to keep them safe and well
As the ark went along on the ocean's swell.
For forty days and forty nights
Water and sky were the only sights.

At the end of that time, the rain it stopped falling
"Lets look for land now!" all the animals were calling.
When a dove flew away and came back with a leaf,
Land should be nearby was Noah's firm belief.
Sure enough the ark found land and stopped upon a hill.
After floating for so long, it seemed strange to be so still.
"Now we must give thanks to God and open up the ark,
To unload all the animals before it gets too dark."
Out went all the creatures, two by two by two.
All eager to go near and far to start their lives anew.

God looked down and spoke aloud to Noah's family,
"Go out into the world again for now you can be free.
This promise I will give to you and keep it for all time
To destroy the world again would be a dreadful crime.
Never ever again will this happen, I shall vow,
And I'll always keep this promise that I've made to you now.
To remind you of this I'll put a rainbow up on high
To see when rain falls and the sun shines in the sky.
So take care of the world, for it is yours always
From today until the very end of all our days."

REFLECTION

Every time you see a rainbow it will remind you of God's promise that he would never destroy the world again.

Prayer

Thank you Lord for the world you have given us. For all the animals, birds, fish and other living creatures on the earth. Thank too for the beautiful rainbow that reminds us of the very special promise you made to us all.

Amen

Song   Rise and shine   (Alleluya, 74: *A&C Black*)

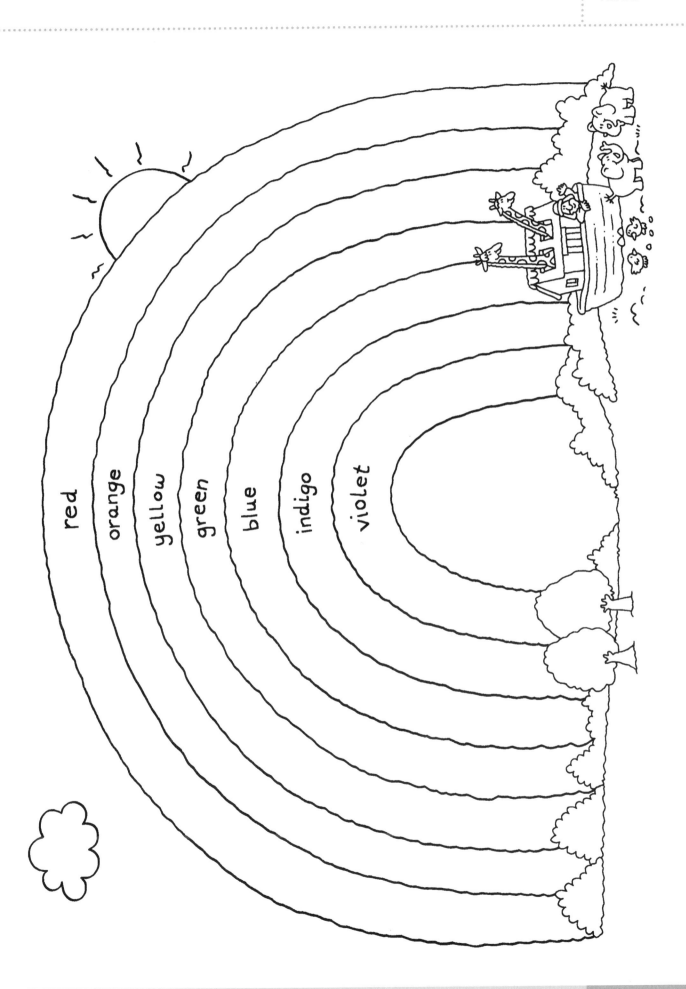

The Good Samaritan

 AIM: To encourage children to see the value in being cheerful and friendly to others.

PREPARATION

- Photcopy 'The Good Samaritan' (page 31) on to paper or card then cut into separate pictures.

■ INTRODUCTION

In the Bible there are some special stories called parables. Jesus told these parables when he wanted to talk to people about how they should live their lives. This parable is the story of The Good Samaritan.

You may wish to add details to set the story in the context of a hot middle-eastern country before the times of motorised transport or even bicycles!

■ STORY

There was once a man travelling along a desert road. (Place man on OHP.)

Suddenly a gang of thieves jumped out and attacked and robbed him. They left the man very badly injured by the side of the road. (Lay man down.)

Later that day another man walked by. This man was a priest. (Place second man on OHP, as if walking past.) *You might have thought he would stop to help, but did he? No he did not. He passed by quickly in case he should be robbed too.* (Remove second man.)

An hour or so after this, another stranger came walking by. (Place third man on OHP.) *He was a religious man who was very well thought of in his town and helped at services in the temple. So do you think he helped? You might have expected him to, but sadly he did not. He glanced quickly at the injured man by the side of the road, and then hurried away thinking only of his own safety.* (Remove third man.)

The next person to travel along the road was a man from another country. The country was called Samaria, so the man was known as a Samaritan. No one thought much of Samaritans and often people were quite unpleasant to them. (Place Samaritan and his donkey on OHP.) *The Samaritan saw the injured man, and went across to see if he could help. He soon realised that the man was very badly injured, so he bathed his wounds and then put the man on his donkey and took him to the nearest town.* (Put injured man on donkey.)

When they reached the town he took the man to an inn. He left the innkeeper enough money to care for the injured man while he regained his health and strength.

■ REFLECTION

Which of the three men do you think was a good friend to the injured man? Was it the priest, the man who helped at the temple, or the man from Samaria that most people had not liked?

Accept answers from the children.

It is always easier to help a good friend than it is to help someone that you don't particularly like. The Samaritan was caring enough to help an enemy and to put himself in danger while doing so.

Jesus told this story to help people to understand the importance of being a 'good neighbour' to others.

Prayer

Dear Lord,
Please help us to remember the importance of being a good neighbour.
Help us to be kind and caring towards everyone that we meet.

Amen

Song

When I needed a neighbour   (Someone's Singing, Lord, 35: *A&C Black*)

The Good Samaritan

The sun and the wind

➡ **AIM: To encourage children to remain calm, courteous and cooperative.**

PREPARATION

■ Photocopy 'The sun and the wind' (page 33) on to paper or card then cut into separate pictures to be used as silhouettes on the OHP.

▪ INTRODUCTION

I wonder what you do when you want something. Do you ever get cross and end up in a temper trying to get your own way? Some people do; though I feel quite sure that none of you would like to behave like that. Perhaps you think about what you want and why you want it, and find a far gentler way to go about getting it. Today we are going to hear a story about how it can be far more effective to do things in a gentle way.

▪ STORY

(Place sun and wind on OHP.) *One day the wind, who was a rather bad tempered bullying character, said to the sun, "I bet I am stronger than you and I can prove it. Do you see that man down there enjoying his walk? I can make him take his coat off."* (Place man wearing coat on OHP.)

The sun just smiled. He was used to hearing the wind boasting and took little notice of it. (Remove sun.) *The wind started to blow at the man, he blew and he blew. Trees started to bend in the wind.* (Add tree to picture.) *The man shivered and pulled his coat around himself. The wind blew even harder, so hard in fact that the branches started breaking off the trees.* (Add broken branches to picture.) *The man did his coat up tightly. The wind blew and blew but it was no good, he just couldn't blow hard enough to take the man's coat off. The sun just smiled.*

Seeing this the wind was crosser than ever.
"I might not have managed to make the man take off his coat but you certainly couldn't do any better. You're far too kind and gentle to make him do anything." The sun smiled again and said, "We'll see." (Remove bent tree and broken branches from picture.) *Then the smiling sun shone brightly through the clear blue sky.* (Add sun to picture.)

The man continued to walk but soon found he was getting rather warm so he unbuttoned his coat. A few minutes later he felt so warm that he took it off. Change man with coat for man without one. He was pleased that it was turning out to be such a pleasant day. The sun smiled at the wind and quietly said, "Sometimes it is far better to be gentle than it is to try and force things your way." The wind went away sulkily to think about what the sun had told him.

▪ REFLECTION

Which of the characters did you like better, the sun or the wind?

Accept answer – which hopefully will be 'the sun'. If time allows, you could further discuss the way in which the story relates to the lives of the children. You could for example ask for any instances in which the pupils used a gentle approach to achieve something.

Prayer

Dear God,
We give you thanks for making us able to deal with situations in a calm way. For voices that can be gentle and kind. For the ability to think about others as well as ourselves and for knowing that you will always be with us to help us deal with difficult events.

Amen

♫
Song

I love the sun   (Someone's Singing, Lord, 12: *A&C Black*)

The Creation

 **AIM: To develop children's awareness of the world around them:
light and dark, plants and animals, people.**

PREPARATION

■ If you are planning to use an OHP, photocopy 'The Creation' (page 35) and cut out
the silhouettes.

▤ INTRODUCTION

Who likes making models? (Show of hands.) *Would anyone like to tell us about the very
best model they have ever made.* (Accept three or four responses.)
*Today I am going to tell you the story of how the Bible says the world was made. It is rather
like a model-making story – but of course it isn't just a model in the story, it is about the
whole of our world. To help me to tell the story I am going to choose some children to put
the pictures in place.* (Choose one child per picture. Start with OHP switched off.)

▤ STORY

*Before the world was made there was nothing but darkness. God decided to make a world so
on the first day he made light to shine through the darkness.* (Ask child to switch on OHP.)
*He was pleased with the light he created and made light and dark times, calling them day
and night.*
On the second day God made the sky and put clouds in it. (Ask a child to place cloud at
the top of the screen.)
*The third day God looked at his world, which as yet had no land, just water. That day he
gave the earth areas of dry land and areas of ocean. Soon trees and flowers would begin to
grow.* (Ask child to place tree in centre of picture.)
On the fourth day God put the sun, moon and stars into place. (Ask children to place sun
on the screen.)
*The next day was the fifth day. On this day God begin to put creatures into the world. He
put fish in the sea, birds in the sky and all sorts of animals on the dry land.* (Ask children to
place fish, bird and animals on appropriate places.)
*On the sixth day God made people. He began with a man called Adam and a woman called
Eve.* (Children to add man and woman to complete the picture at the bottom of the
screen.)
*On the seventh day God stopped and rested and looked at the wonderful world he had
created. As he admired the world he decided that the seventh day should always be a special
one. People should always use the seventh day as a day to rest from their usual work and
use the day to think about God, to say prayers, and to be thankful for all the beautiful
things in the world around them.*

▤ REFLECTION

Ask for responses concerning the seventh day eg. which day do children in your school
think is the day of rest? This may vary according to the religions represented among pupils
and their families.
You may wish to mention that other religions have varying creation stories and that the
important thing is that we appreciate and care for the world in which we live.

Prayer

Dear God,
*Thank you, for the wonderful world in which we live. For the sun in the day and the moon
and stars at night. For the land and the water. For the marvellous creatures all around the
world; the fish that swim, the birds that fly and the many types of animals and insects. Most
of all thank you for putting us in the world. Help us to do our best to care for the world and
all the creatures in it.*
Amen

Song

God who put the stars in space   (Someone's Singing, Lord, 47: *A&C Black*)
or
Think of a world without any flowers   (Someone's Singing, Lord, 15: *A&C Black*)

Andrew Brodie: Assembly Today KS1 © A&C Black Publishers Ltd. 2005

The Creation

Nests, eggs and baby birds

 AIM: To consider the wonder of new life.

PREPARATION

■ Prepare for this assembly by photocopying and cutting out the silhouettes on page 37.

■ ASSEMBLY

In spring time the birds are busy making their nests ready for the mother birds to lay their eggs. They hunt around for materials to make the nests: twigs and leaves and sometimes bits of grass. Some birds line the insides of the nest with their own feathers to make the nest soft and comfortable.

(Place silhouette of nest on OHP.) *Many birds build their nests in trees, high off the ground so that foxes or other animals can't get to the eggs. Some birds build their nests in bushes or hedges where they are well hidden from other animals and from us humans. Some birds build their nests on the ground but they hide them so well in long grass or in heather that we can't see them unless we look really carefully.*

(Add eggs to nest.) *When the nests are ready the mother birds lay their eggs, then the birds sit on them to keep them warm for days and days and days. Sometimes the mother bird and the father bird will take it in turns to sit on the eggs. Whatever happens they have to keep the eggs warm because inside the eggs, baby chicks are growing.* (Add bird to the nest.)

While the birds are sitting on the eggs the baby chicks are developing inside the eggs, getting stronger and stronger until one day they can peck their way out through the eggshells. Once they come out of the shells the baby birds are not ready to fly but they still need looking after by the father and mother birds. This is when the adult birds are really busy. They fly off to collect some food, then they bring it back to feed the babies, then they fly off to get some more because the babies are always hungry. (Remove bird and eggs and place baby birds on nest.)

The adult birds feed the baby birds for days and days and days. Every day the baby birds grow a little stronger and every day their feathers grow a little bigger until, one day, they are ready to learn to fly. They are still not adults themselves but they are big enough to leave the nest and go out into the big wide world.

■ REFLECTION

Prayer

Dear God,
Please help all the birds who are making nests and laying eggs and looking after babies. We thank you for the birds and the spring time.

Amen

Song

A little tiny bird   (Someone's Singing, Lord, 24: *A&C Black*)

The ugly duckling 1

AIM: This deals well with the subject of bullying. In 'real life' things do not always work out so well and children will be aware of this. Nevertheless, they should be able to extract two key morals from the story: that bullies are not always right and that individuals should try to feel confident about themselves.

PREPARATION

■ Prepare for this assembly by photocopying and cutting out the silhouettes on page 39.

■ INTRODUCTION

Today's story is all about bullies. Bullies are people who are mean to other people. They haven't learnt yet that it is better to be kind to other people.

■ STORY

One sunny spring time a mother duck and a father duck built a good, strong, safe nest in some reeds at the edge of a large lake. (Place lake and reeds on OHP.) Lots of other birds and animals lived on, in or near the lake. There were water voles (which are a bit like rats and some people call them water rats); there were tall herons, beautiful white swans, kingfishers; and there were lots and lots of ducks. The lake was a very busy place so the two ducks built their nest away from the other ducks' nests and very well hidden in amongst the reeds.

Mother duck laid her eggs, then she sat on them patiently, keeping them warm. (Place mother duck on reeds.) Day after day she sat there, just occasionally slipping away to find some food, then coming back and sitting still to keep her eggs safe and warm. She had nine eggs but she couldn't count so she didn't notice, when she came back from finding some food one day, that an extra egg was in the nest with all the rest. She didn't even notice that the extra egg was bigger than all the others.

So now mother duck was sitting on ten eggs, keeping them safe and warm. Day after day she sat there, then after about four weeks of sitting, the shells on the eggs started to break and little ducklings pushed and squeezed and forced themselves out of the eggs and sat in the nest looking around at the world for the first time. Mother duck was so proud; she was even proud of the biggest, ugliest duckling who had squeezed its way out of the biggest egg. "You are an ugly duckling!" she said, "but I love you anyway."

Day after day mother duck looked after those ducklings, finding them food and sometimes giving them rides on her back when she was swimming on the lake. Sometimes she swam along and the ducklings followed along behind her in a long line with the big ugly one at the end. (Add all ducklings to OHP.) The ducklings grew bigger and stronger. The ugly duckling grew bigger and stronger than all the others...and uglier too! "You are an ugly duckling!" mother duck would say, "but I love you anyway."

But the other ducklings didn't love the ugly duckling and neither did the other adult ducks who lived nearby. "You are an ugly duckling!" they would say. "We don't love you, even if your mother does. Go away! Go away!" The ugly duckling was frightened and upset.

■ REFLECTION

Who are the bullies in this story? Why did they bully the ugly duckling? We'll carry on with this story in our next assembly.

Prayer

*Dear God,
Please don't let us behave like the bullies in the story. Please don't let us be mean to someone just because they are a bit different to us.*   *Amen*

Song

Nobody's a nobody   (Everyone's Singing, Lord, 31: *A&C Black*)

The ugly duckling 2

 AIM: To promote self confidence and lack of fear of others and to encourage children not to cause fear in others.

PREPARATION

■ Photocopy 'The ugly duckling 2' (page 42) on to paper or card then cut into separate pictures to be used as silhouettes on the OHP.

■ INTRODUCTION

Do you remember what happened at the end of the story in the last assembly? Accept answers from the pupils.

Let's hear the next part of the story.

■ STORY

The poor ugly duckling was being bullied by the other ducklings and even by some of the adult ducks just because he looked different from the others. He was bigger than them and his feathers were ugly because they were all grey and brown and sprouted out from his body in tufts. The other ducklings had pretty feathers that were soft and mottled with different shades of brown. "You are an ugly duckling!" they would say. "We don't love you, even if your mother does. Go away! Go away!"

The ugly duckling was frightened and upset. He didn't know what to do. He climbed out of the water, all on his own, and walked along the shore of the lake. But the other ducklings swam along the lake near to the shore, calling to him: "Ugly duckling; ugly duckling! Go away!"

So the ugly duckling turned away from the lake and walked and walked and walked, all on his own. He walked with his head down, looking sadly at the ground. He walked and walked and walked, until it began to get dark then he looked up and realised that he just didn't know where he was. He was completely lost. He couldn't see his lake, he couldn't see the other ducklings and, worst of all, he couldn't see his mum. He was very sad.

The ugly duckling looked around carefully. He couldn't see the lake but he could see some reeds in the distance and reeds meant there must be water so he decided to walk towards them. When he got to the reeds he saw that there was a very long straight stretch of water – it was a canal. He lowered himself into the water and began to float, paddling himself gently along; it felt lovely not to be walking. It was getting darker and darker so the ugly duckling decided to go and rest in the reeds for the night; it would be safe in there even if he did miss his dear mother duck.

The next day when the ugly duckling woke up the sun was shining and it was a most beautiful summer's day. The water in the canal sparkled brightly and, although the ugly duckling still missed his mother, he felt much better. He knew that he couldn't find his way back to the lake so he decided that he would stay at the canal. There was nobody here to be mean to him.

Day after day, the ugly duckling swam up and down the canal and night after night he sheltered in amongst the reeds. He was a bit lonely but he was quite happy because nobody was being mean to him. Day after day, until the summer turned to autumn and the autumn turned to winter and, at last, the winter turned to spring.

One fine spring day, the ugly duckling looked up into the sky as he heard the sounds of strong wings beating. He was amazed to see two big beautiful swans flying over the canal. Then they turned and flew over it again. He thought that they looked magnificent, but then he became very frightened because they were coming down from the sky straight towards him. 'Oh no,' he thought to himself, 'they are going to call me names like the ducklings on the lake did.'

Andrew Brodie: Assembly Today KS1 © A&C Black Publishers Ltd. 2005

The ugly duckling 2

The two big swans skidded along the surface of the canal and then came to a stop right in front of the ugly duckling. (Place two swans on OHP.)
"We came down to see you," one of them said. "Do you live here?"
"Yes," replied the ugly duckling.
"We didn't know there were any other swans living near here," said the swans. The ugly duckling didn't understand.
"What do you mean 'other swans'?" he asked.
"We thought we were the only swans around here but now there's you. We're very pleased to see you."
"But, I'm not a swan!" said the ugly duckling.
"Of course you are," said the other swans kindly.
The ugly duckling swam to the edge of the canal and climbed out onto the bank. He found some water where no reeds were growing, where there was no water weed, where the water was still and calm. He leaned over the water and looked at the surface and it was like looking into a mirror. For the first time he saw his own reflection but he didn't see the ugly duckling he was expecting to see; he saw the most beautiful swan in the whole world.

He was so excited. He climbed back into the water and stretched out his wings and for the first time he realised that his wings were covered in beautiful snowy white feathers, not the little tufty grey and brown feathers that he had had before. He flapped and flapped his wings and, before long, he was able to rise up into the sky and look down on his canal and his two new friends.
"I'm not an ugly duckling, I'm a beautiful swan!" he called.

He flew in big circles round and round the spot where the two other swans were floating on the canal. (Add flying swan to OHP.) *From up here he could see for miles. Suddenly he spotted a shining stretch of water a long way away. He could fly so strongly now that he decided to go to see this water. When he got close to it he saw that it was a lake – it was his lake, where he used to live. He flew lower and lower until he was skimming just above the surface of the lake. With long beats of his giant white wings he was an amazing sight for all the birds who lived on the lake.*
"Look, mother!" called some young ducks. "Look at that beautiful swan!"

▮ REFLECTION

You may like to pose the following questions with a view to encouraging the children to understand the morals of the story:

Who do you think the young ducks were? Who was their mother?
What did they think of the swan? Do you think that they ever found out that the swan was the creature that they used to call the ugly duckling?
Do you think that the beautiful swan recognised the young ducks and their mother? What did he think of them?

Prayer
Dear God,
Help us to be confident of ourselves just like the ugly duckling who found that really he was a beautiful swan. Help us not to be frightened by people who might try to bully us. Help us not to bully other people.

Amen

Song   Nobody's a nobody   (Everyone's Singing, Lord, 31: *A&C Black*)

The ugly duckling 2

Andrew Brodie: Assembly Today KS1 © A&C Black Publishers Ltd. 2005

Helping hands

AIM: To help children appreciate their hands and the importance of using them wisely.

PREPARATION

■ If you are planning to use an OHP, photocopy 'Helping hands' (page 44) on to acetate.

INTRODUCTION

Today I need a hand.

(Place acetate of hand outline on OHP.)

Mrs _____ , could you give me a hand?

Mrs _____ comes to OHP but her hand doesn't fit.

Mr _____ , could you give me a hand?

Mr _____ comes to OHP but his hand doesn't fit.

If time allows, continue with a couple more adults then try a child. Hopefully the first child's hand won't fit exactly but after one or two children you will find a child whose hand fits perfectly.

I've found a hand that fits. Let's give _____ a hand. Clap!

ACTIVITY

Let's think about hands. What can we do with our hands? Some people do bad things with their hands but most people do good things with their hands. Let's think about bad things first. Can anybody tell me about bad things that people do with their hands?

The children will probably suggest hitting or scratching or stealing as examples of bad things that hands do. We suggest that this part of the assembly is dealt with quickly so that the positive aspects rather than the negative aspects are stressed. Clearly the children may make some suggestions regarding hitting by named individuals but a positive assembly is not the time for this to be discussed and the issues should be passed over quickly.

Now, let's think about good things because good things are much nicer. Can anybody tell me about good things that people do with their hands?

Hopefully there will be many suggestions: writing, drawing, painting, stroking a cat, shaking hands.

Let's all do something good with our hands now. Turn to your neighbour and shake hands with him or her. It would be good to give a nice smile at the same time.

REFLECTION

Prayer

Dear God,
Please help us to do good things with our hands. Help us not to be tempted to do bad things.

Amen

Song   The building song   (Alleluya, 59: *A&C Black*)

Helping hands

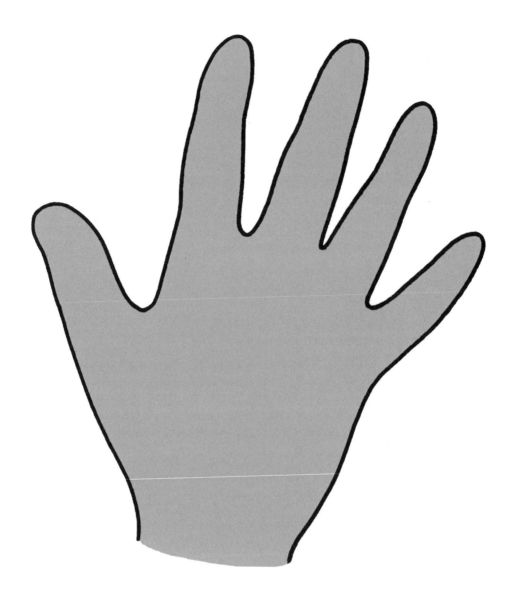

Planting the seeds

 AIM: To help children be aware of plants and their care.

PREPARATION

- You will need to photocopy and cut out the silhouettes on page 46 ready to use at appropriate points in this assembly. (You can also use some of these silhouettes in the autumn term when telling the story of the enormous turnip.)
- You may like to have some garden tools available to demonstrate the digging and the raking.

■ INTRODUCTION

At this time of year the days are getting longer and the nights are getting shorter. You can go out and play in the garden in the evening; some people like to go out in the garden and work in the evening. Perhaps someone in your family works in the garden. What sort of jobs do people do in their gardens?

Hopefully the pupils will respond with suggestions such as lawn-mowing, digging, weeding…

■ STORY

One day in April a man called Eric went out to work in his garden. (Place Eric on OHP.) *Eric loved to work in his garden. His wife, Peggy, quite liked working in the garden as well. She liked cutting the grass.* (Place Peggy and lawn mower on OHP.) *She said that when she was cutting the grass the world was very peaceful – the lawn mower made a lot of noise but it made so much noise that she couldn't hear the telephone and she couldn't hear the children, Jack and Jenny, arguing with each other!* (Add Jack and Jenny to OHP.)

Eric's favourite job was planting seeds and looking after them until they grew into beautiful flowers or tasty vegetables. First he had to dig the garden to turn over all the soil. (Place spade in Eric's hand.) *When he was digging he could pull out the weeds, then he could stand back and admire the lovely brown soil that looked so fresh. Once he had dug all the soil he would get the garden rake and pull it backwards and forwards over the soil, breaking the soil into small pieces and pulling out any large stones.* (Swap spade for rake.) *Eric raked so much that the soil became very fine and the patch of garden looked like a neat brown carpet.*

One particular day, Eric decided to plant some vegetable seeds. Can you think of the type of seeds that he might have planted? Well, he planted carrot seeds, pea seeds, bean seeds but, most importantly, he planted turnip seeds because he loved turnips.

After he had planted the seeds, he gave them all a small amount of water by sprinkling it from his watering can. He had to remember to water them every day, if they needed water. Why did he have to water them some days and not others?

Some days it was sunny and some days there was rain. Warmth from the sun and water from the rain are exactly what seeds need to help them grow. Day after day, Eric looked after the seeds. Then, one day, he became very excited because he saw some little tiny green shoots beginning to appear from out of the soil. Day after day, he looked after the little shoots and they grew bigger and stronger. His seeds were growing into strong healthy plants. Eric was looking forward to eating the vegetables but he would have to wait for quite a long time because vegetables take a long time to grow.

■ REFLECTION

Prayer

Dear God, We thank you for gardens, for beautiful flowers and for tasty vegetables. Thank you for sending the sun and rain to help all the plants grow.

Amen

Song   Think of a world without any flowers   (Someone's Singing, Lord, 15: *A&C Black*)

Planting the seeds

The hare and the tortoise

 AIM: To encourage children to recognise and value their own skills and those of others.

PREPARATION

- Photocopy 'The hare and the tortoise' sheets 1 and 2 (page 49 and 50) on to paper or card then cut into separate pictures to be used as silhouettes on the OHP.

POSSIBLE INTRODUCTION

As with all the stories in this book, you may well like to tell this story and the introduction in your own words, following the structure set out below.

In the summer term, if we are lucky with the weather, you have lots of chances to go outside at break times and for PE lessons. Sometimes it's good fun to have races with your friends. We all try very hard to win when we are racing and it doesn't matter if we don't win, so long as we try hard, we don't cheat and we enjoy ourselves.

Some people are very good at winning races, but they don't show off about it although they are very proud because they are so good at running. Other people are very good at winning races, but they do show off about it. They say things like, "I'm the best," or "I always win."

You may like to ask the children some questions:

Put your hand up if you think that you are good at winning races.
Put your hand up if you think that you are too slow to win races.
How many people like having races?
How many people don't like having races?

Clearly, sensitivity is needed in response to the questions and to the answers. Children with disabilities, in particular, may be very conscious of their limitations in relation to competitive sport. However, as you know, the moral of Aesop's fable about a hare and a tortoise who compete in a race is that the fastest person does not always win in the end; he may win many, many races but the slower person may do very well by working hard, trying hard and keeping going.

STORY

Today's story is about two runners. One of them was a very fast runner indeed. (Place the picture of the hare on to the OHP.) *The hare was very fast. He won lots of races and because he kept winning he kept asking all the other animals to race with him. He asked the lion, who was also a very fast runner.* (Place the picture of the lion on to the OHP.) *So the hare and the lion had a race but, guess who won? … the hare won the race.*

The hare asked the dog, who was also a very fast runner. (Place the picture of the dog on to the OHP). *So the hare and the dog had a race but, guess who won? The hare won the race. Remove the dog and the lion from the screen.*

Lots of animals raced with the hare, but every time the hare won. And every time he won he said, "I'm the best; I always win!" The other animals were getting very fed up with this.
It was no fun having a race if you could never win and it was very annoying listening to the hare showing off about it. The hare kept asking other animals to race with him but now they always said things like, "I can't, I've just washed my fur," or "Sorry, I could win but I've got a lot to do today."

One day the animals were all gathered together for a chat. The hare kept asking each one, "Will you race with me?" "No!" He went from one animal to another. "Will you race with me?" "No!"

Suddenly a little voice piped up, "I'll race with you." All the animals looked around to see who had volunteered to race with the hare. Who could it be? It must be someone very brave and extremely fast. Then they all spotted who it was. It was the slow, old tortoise. (Place the picture of the tortoise on to the OHP.) *All the animals laughed. "You can't possibly win,"* they said. (Remove the hare and the tortoise from the screen.)

The animals decided to get the race ready. They made it a very long route. It would start at the bridge. (Place the picture of the bridge on to the OHP.) *The hare and the tortoise would have to run all the way around the big hill.* (Place the picture of the hill on to the OHP). *Then they would have to run all the way back to the bridge.* (Remove the bridge and the hill from the screen.)

The hare and the tortoise got ready to run. (Place the hare and the tortoise on the screen. *The lion shouted, "Go!" The race began. The hare started off really fast, so fast he was out of sight in no time.* (Remove the hare from the screen.) *The tortoise just plodded on slowly.* (Remove the tortoise from the screen.) *Soon, the hare was running round the hill. He got to the other side and decided that perhaps he should sit down and rest. He made himself comfortable and soon nodded off to sleep.* (Place the sleeping hare on the screen. Pause, then remove the hare and put on the tortoise.)

The tortoise just plodded on slowly. Eventually he got to the hill; slowly he walked round the hill. He saw the hare asleep and went past quietly so that he didn't wake the hare up. The tortoise just plodded on slowly. Two hours later, the tortoise was still plodding on slowly but he could see the finish line! (Place the finish line on the screen. Pause, then remove the finish line and put on the hare.)

It was then that the hare woke up. "I suppose I'd better get on with this race. I wonder where that tortoise is," he said to himself. He started running again, really fast just like he always ran. "I'll beat him by miles," he said. "I'm the best; I always win!"

The hare ran even faster and, suddenly, he could see the finish line. He could see all the other animals standing near the finish line and they were cheering! "They must be cheering for me!" he shouted, "because I'm the best; I always win!"

But they weren't cheering for the hare. Who were they cheering for? The tortoise. They were cheering for the tortoise because the tortoise had won the race. The hare ran over the finish line and realised that, for the first time, he had not won a race.
"Well done," he said to the tortoise. "I was silly. I'll never show off again."
"Thank you," said the tortoise. "Neither will I."

■ REFLECTION

That story was written by a man called Aesop, over two thousand five hundred years ago. We can learn from the story. We can learn not to show off. We can learn that everybody has their own skills – the hare's skill was that he could run fast; the tortoise's skill was that he didn't give up. Sometimes we say that a person has a gift; we mean that that person has a particular skill. What do you think your gift or skill is?

Prayer

Dear God,
Help us to use our own skills in school and at home. Help us to know that everybody has a skill. Help us to respect one another.

Amen

Song
The best gift (BBC Come and Praise, 59)

The hare and the tortoise 1

The hare and the tortoise 2

finish

Andrew Brodie: Assembly Today KS1 © A&C Black Publishers Ltd. 2005

Mingle, mingle

AIM: To promote good manners and friendship between individuals in the school community.

PREPARATION

- If yours is a large school it is useful, though not essential, to present this assembly with only half the school present. It is important that members of staff are present.

INTRODUCTION

By the summer term all children should be settled into school very well. There will still be some who are very quiet and introverted while others are totally the opposite. The assembly outlined below has worked very successfully in encouraging the introverted children to speak up, even if only briefly, and the outgoing children to think a little more about other people. This assembly is particularly successful where the hall is not completely full – perhaps if the assembly is for half of the school or for just some of the classes.

INTRODUCTION SCRIPT

I know everybody in the school. I know the teachers, the assistants and all the other adults…and I know all of you too. I am very lucky. When I meet people I know I say things like, "Hello Ashley, how are you?" or "Good morning, Mrs Jones. Lovely day, isn't it?" or "Hello, Mr Singh, isn't this rain horrible?" Sometimes, though, I meet people for the very first time. It's more difficult then to think of things to say, but I might say, "Hello, my name is…I am a teacher at…"
What do you say when you meet people for the first time? Put your hand up if you can think of what you might say.
If there are no responses, you could make suggestions such as *"Hello, my name is… I like playing football,"* or *"Hello, my name is… I like drawing pictures."*

ASSEMBLY

Today you are going to meet someone new for the very first time. In fact, you will meet lots of people you have never met before. You will have seen these people before, lots of times, but you have never spoken to them. Have a good look around the room. Somewhere in the room there is somebody you have seen before but never spoken to. Perhaps this person is in the class above or the class next door or the class below yours. Perhaps this person is a teacher or an assistant.
In a moment I am going to ask you to get up from the floor and go over and meet someone who you have never spoken to before. When you meet this person, say 'hello', then tell them something about you – what you like or what you don't like or what you do. Of course, the most important thing is to be polite when you speak to the person so try hard to say something nice.
Remember, we are all going to do this so we will have to speak fairly quietly. When I clap twice, please stop speaking. Are you ready? Go and meet someone new.
Allow a short time for the children to move and speak, then stop them.
Now, you've met one person, go and meet somebody else.
This can be repeated several times. Eventually, when you decide to stop the activity, you may wish to ask the children to sit down where they are. When they leave the hall, they can simply be called out class by class.

REFLECTION

Prayer

Dear God, Please help us to meet new people. Help us to listen to what other people tell us and help us to speak clearly to them. Please help us to be polite to everybody we meet.

Amen

Song

If I had a hammer   (Someone's Singing, Lord, 37: *A&C Black*)

Every little helps

AIM: This assembly should focus on how important it is for everyone to contribute to whatever is happening, and that their contribution really is important even if it doesn't seem to be.

PREPARATION

■ If you are planning to use an OHP, photocopy 'Every little helps' (page 53) on to acetate.

INTRODUCTION

Introduce the assembly by saying something like:

Today we are going to think about how important it is for everyone to play their part in group events. Sometimes you may think that what you need to do isn't very important and it doesn't matter whether you play your part or not. I am going to tell you a story about what could happen when people don't do their jobs properly.

STORY

It was the day of the tidy village competition. The judges would be arriving at two o'clock that afternoon. The village looked very tidy; every garden, every path and every grass verge was looking at its best. The infants school was in the centre of the village. The children there had a very important job to do – they had to keep the playground completely free of litter. So that day it was vital that everybody was especially careful to make sure that the only place any rubbish went was in the litter bin.

Jay was enjoying playing in the playground when a scrap of paper fell out of his pocket. He should have picked it up and taken it to the bin, but he was so busy playing with his friends that he didn't bother. He thought just one piece of paper really wouldn't matter.

The result of the tidy village competition was announced the following week. The children at school were looking forward to hearing the result. They felt quite sure their village must have won. To their great disappointment it hadn't won. The judges had been very pleased with most parts of the village but said that the litter scattered in the school playground had rather spoiled the look of the village.

At first Jay couldn't believe it. It wasn't his fault, after all he had only let one small scrap of paper fall on the ground. Then he realised that if everybody in the school had also dropped just one small thing then of course it would have made the playground look terrible. He knew then just how important it was for everyone to make the effort as every little helps.

REFLECTION

Ask the children what they think they have learned from the story. Emphasise the fact that the assembly was mainly about the importance of playing your part. Can the children think of any group events they have been asked to take part in and what their part was? Explain that next assembly you will be thinking about the issue of litter, so you will be asking them to remember the story for next time.

Prayer

Dear God,
Help us to play our part fully in all that we do. We thank you for giving us friends, family and the school community to be a valued part of _____ .

Amen

♫
Song

He gave me eyes so I could see   (Someone's Singing, Lord, 19: *A&C Black*)

Every little helps

A clean and tidy world

AIM: To encourage children to look after the world by disposing of litter sensibly and to appreciate others whose jobs involve keeping the world clean.

PREPARATION

- Ideally this assembly should follow the 'Every little helps' assembly and if time the same story can be read again.
- If you are planning to use an OHP, photocopy 'A clean and tidy world' (page 55) on to acetate.

INTRODUCTION

Do you remember what happened in the story you heard in our last assembly? Allow children to remind you about the story. You may wish to read it again if there is time. *Last time we thought about how we should all play our part in things. Today we are going to think about how important it is to make sure that all our rubbish goes in the litter bins.*

ASSEMBLY

Where can you find litter bins in and around our school?

Accept responses/discuss.

Where do you put any rubbish when you are not in school?

Accept responses/discuss.

Why do you think it is very important to make sure that our litter is not just dropped on the ground?

Accept responses – particularly encourage responses concerning likely damage to other creatures.

REFLECTION

I hope you will all remember the importance of throwing our rubbish away properly. I'm sure you will all remember to use the bins today, that's the easy part. What is much harder is to make sure you keep using bins every day, and not just in school but at home and when you are out. If you can't see a bin then keep your litter until you do. If we all remember what to do with our litter then we will all be helping to make the world a cleaner, tidier place. We will also be helping to keep all of God's creatures safe from the harm our litter could do to them.

Prayer

Dear Lord,
Thank you for the wonderful world we live it. Help us to keep the world a lovely place by putting our litter in the bin.
Thank you for all the wonderful creatures that live in the world. Help us to try to keep them safer by putting our litter in the bin.
Thank you for the work of all the people who work with the rubbish we throw away every day, for those who empty our bins at home, at school and on the roads and streets nearby.
Amen

♫
Song

Milk bottle tops and paper bags   (Someone's Singing, Lord, 17: *A&C Black*)

A clean and tidy world

The argument

 AIM: To promote tolerance and understanding of others.

PREPARATION

■ Prepare for this assembly by photocopying 'The argument' (page 57) on to acetate.

■ INTRODUCTION

You could begin the assembly (if appropriate in your school) by first asking which children belong to which religious faith. You can do this with a simple show of hands from those who wish to share this information with the group. Introduce the assembly by saying something like:

Everyone is different, and different religions believe slightly different things. Today's assembly is about three children who all thought their idea was the only correct one. Listen carefully to the story to see who was right.

■ STORY

One hot summer's day three children sat in the shade beneath a large oak tree. They were talking about their religious beliefs and ended up arguing. Their teacher came across to see what the problem was.

One of the children said, "Our families worship different Gods – but who is worshipping the real one?"

The teacher said, "Look up and tell me what you can see."

The first child looked up and said, "I can see some large branches, lots of lovely green leaves and a nest nearly hidden by the leaves." The next child looked up and said, " From where I am sitting I can see leaves moving in the breeze, a little bit of blue sky and a squirrel balancing on a branch." The third child said, " I can see interesting patterns on the tree trunk, a bird landing on a branch and some acorns starting to grow among the leaves."

The teacher smiled and said to the three children, "You are all sitting under the same old oak tree that is protecting you from the heat of the sun, but when you looked up you all saw something different. I hope that will help you to understand who is worshipping the real God."

The children looked puzzled at first, but soon realised what the teacher meant.

■ REFLECTION

At this point in the assembly, ask pupils what they think the story is telling them. Accept their contributions then emphasise the lesson in the story. This story shows that we all see things in different ways, even when we are all actually looking at the same thing. The tree in the story represents God. The tree was protecting all the children from the heat of the sun. When the children looked up at the tree they all saw different things. Everything they saw was real, just different. If time, discuss further how this story relates to them and their varying forms of worship.

Prayer

Dear God,
Teach me the wisdom of tolerance. Help me to respect the ideas and beliefs of others and to appreciate their ways of thinking.

Amen

♪
Song

Praise to the Lord our God   (Alleluya, 8: *A&C Black*)

The argument

Looking after ourselves 1

AIM: To encourage pupils to keep themselves safe from harm.

PREPARATION

■ If you are planning to use an OHP, photocopy 'Looking after ourselves' (page 59) and cut into separate pictures.

■ INTRODUCTION

These assemblies are based on the poem 'Story of Johnny Head in Air' by Dr. Heinrich Hoffman (1809 – 1874). When introducing this assembly it is important to encourage the children to identify firstly the people who help to keep them safe in their day to day lives, (parents, carers, teachers etc.). Next, help the pupils to consider ways they help to keep themselves safe and well. (Healthy eating, following safety rules etc.)

■ ASSEMBLY

The Story of Johnny Head-In-Air   (Place shape of Johnny on OHP.)
As he trudg'd along to school,
It was always Johnny's rule
To be looking at the sky
And the clouds that floated by.   (Add clouds to OHP.)
But what just before him lay,
In the way
Johnny never thought about;
So that everyone cried out –
"Look at little Johnny there,
Little Johnny head in air!"
Running just in Johnny's way
Came a little dog one day;   (Place dog on OHP in front of Johnny.)
Johnny's eyes were still astray
Up on high
In the sky;
And he never heard them cry –
"Johnny mind the dog is nigh!"
Bump! Bump!
Down they fell with such a thump!   (Move shape of Johnny as if he has
Dog and Johnny in a lump.   fallen over dog.)
Once with head as high as ever   (Remove dog – place Johnny upright again.)
Johnny walked beside the river.
Johnny watched the swallows trying   (Add birds)
Which was cleverest at flying.
Oh what fun
Johnny watched the bright round sun   (Add clouds with sun moving behind them.)
Going in and coming out.
This was all he thought about.
So he strode and only think,
To the river's very brink
Where the bank was high and steep
And the river very deep.

■ REFLECTION

What do the pupils think is likely to happen next? How could Johnny have looked after himself better? Explain that the poem will be completed in the next assembly.

Prayer

Dear Lord,
As I am growing up help me to stay safe. Help me to use my eyes to see where I am going and my ears to hear things around me. Watch over me every day as I grow and learn how best to keep myself safe.
                                                                            Amen

Song

He gave me eyes so I could see   (Someone's Singing, Lord, 19: *A&C Black*)

Looking after ourselves 2

 AIM: To encourage pupils to keep themselves safe from harm.

PREPARATION

■ If you are planning to use an OHP, photocopy 'Looking after ourselves 2' on to acetate and cut into separate pieces.

◼ INTRODUCTION

Remind children of the issues considered in the previous assembly. Explain that today they will be hearing the second part of the 'Johnny Head-In-Air' poem.

◼ ASSEMBLY

The Story of Johnny Head-In-Air (continued)

So he strode and only think,	(Place Johnny by river banks as
To the river's very brink,	previous assembly had ended)
Where the bank was high and steep	
And the water very deep	
And the fishes in a row	
Stand to see him coming so.	(Add fish)
One step more!	
Oh! Sad to tell!	
Headlong in poor Johnny fell.	(Place Johnny face down in river)
And the fishes in dismay.	
Wagged their tails and ran away.	(Remove fish)
There lay Johnny on his face,	
With his nice red writing case;	
But, as they were passing by,	
Two big men had heard him cry.	(Add men)
And with sticks the two big men	
Hook'd poor Johnny out again.	(Men help Johnny from river)
Oh! You should have seen him shiver,	
When they pulled him from the river.	
He was in a sorry plight!	
Dripping wet and such a fright!	
Wet all over everywhere,	
Clothes, and arms and face, and hair.	
Johnny never will forget	
What it is to be so wet.	
And the fishes, one, two, three,	(Bring back fish)
Are come back again you see;	
Up they came the moment after,	
To enjoy the fun and laughter.	
Each popped out his little head	
And to tease poor Johnny said,	
"Silly little Johnny look,	
You have lost your writing book."	*Heinrich Hoffmann*

◼ REFLECTION

Discuss the consequences of Johnny not looking where he was going, and what might have happened had the men not been walking by.

Prayer

Dear Lord,
As I am growing up help me to stay safe. Thank you for the people who help me to do the things I am unable to do for myself. Watch over me each day as I continue to grow and learn more about the world.

Amen

Song

Hands to work and feet to run   (Someone's Singing, Lord, 21: *A&C Black*)

Andrew Brodie: Assembly Today KS1 © A&C Black Publishers Ltd. 2005

Symbols of world religions

AIM: To raise awareness of the existence of a variety of religions and to promote tolerance and kindness between people.

PREPARATION

■ Photocopy 'Symbols of world religions' (pages 63-64) on to acetate and then cut into separate pictures.

■ INTRODUCTION

You may wish to adapt the assembly to suit the background of your school and the faiths of your pupils. We suggest that you turn out the lights in the hall and light a candle at the front before the children enter.

This assembly could follow 'The argument' (page 56) and you could again begin the assembly (if appropriate in your school) by first asking which children belong to which religious faith.

■ ASSEMBLY

Everyone is different in lots of ways because everyone is special. There are different religions too and different religions believe slightly different things but each one is special. Today we are going to look at some of the symbols of some of the different religions in the world. You will see some symbols that you know and you will probably see some that you have never seen before.

Let's start with a symbol from the Sikh religion. It's called the khanda. Can you see that it shows some curved swords? Can you see the circle? This represents the perfection of God who lasts for ever and ever.

This symbol shows a crescent moon. It is the symbol of the religion called Islam.

Here is a symbol from the Hindu religion. It is called the Om and it represents the whole of life.

This symbol is called the wheel of life. It is from the religion called Buddhism.

This symbol is from the Christian religion. It is a cross and it represents the cross on which Jesus died.

Here is a symbol from Judaism. It is called the Star of David and it may have been the shape of the shield that he carried.

■ REFLECTION

All of the symbols are important to the people of those religions. All the religions are important because they all teach people how to live their lives. One important message that the religions teach is that people should be kind to one another.

Prayer

Dear God,
Help us to be kind to one another in this school. Help us to understand people from other religions. Help us to be kind to all people.

Amen

Song

If I had a hammer   (Someone's Singing, Lord, 37: *A&C Black*)

Symbols of world religions